Oprah Winfrey

by Jill C. Wheeler

visit us at
www.abdopub.com

Published by ABDO & Daughters, an imprint of ABDO
Publishing Company, 4940 Viking Drive, Suite 622, Edina,
Minnesota 55435. Copyright ©2002 by Abdo Consulting
Group, Inc. International copyrights reserved in all countries.
No part of this book may be reproduced in any form without
written permission from the publisher.

Printed in the United States.

Edited by Paul Joseph
Graphic Design: John Hamilton
Cover Design: Mighty Media
Interior Photos: Corbis and AP/Photo

Library of Congress Cataloging-in-Publication Data

Wheeler, Jill C., 1964-
    Oprah Winfrey / Jill C. Wheeler
        p.   cm. — (Breaking Barriers)
    Includes index.
    Summary: Focuses on the accomplishments of the television talk
show host, actor, and producer who is one of the most recognized
females in the world.
    ISBN 1-57765-319-X
    1. Winfrey, Oprah—Juvenile literature. 2. Television
personalities—United States—Juvenile literature. 3. Motion picture
actors and actresses—United States—Biography—Juvenile literature.
I. Title. II. Series: Wheeler, Jill C., 1964- Breaking Barriers.
    PN1992.4.W56W54 2002
    791.45'028'092
    [B]—DC21

98-29313
CIP
AC

Contents

"See, Daddy?" 4

Entertaining the Chickens 8

Problem Child..14

Rules, Rules, & More Rules 20

The Broadcast World 26

A Show of Her Own................................32

A New Style of Talk Show 36

Making Movies 40

Personal Battles 44

Writing Books...50

Giving Back 52

What's Next for Oprah? 56

Timeline 60

Where on the Web? 61

Glossary 62

Index 64

"See, Daddy?"

*T*he crowd at the 1987 Tennessee State University commencement buzzed with excitement. The speaker that day was a special woman. She had left the school without a degree. Eleven years later, she had returned to get it.

A lot had happened in those 11 years. The woman had become the host of a daytime television talk show. In just a few years, the show had become so popular that TV stations around the country began to broadcast it. She was in the living rooms of millions of people every day.

The speaker told the crowd that day that she had never forgotten that she left college without her degree. Nor had her father. "Every time I come home, my dad says, 'You need that degree,'" she told the crowd. "So this is a special day for my dad."

Oprah Winfrey

It also was a special day for the university. Their guest speaker was among the richest entertainers in the industry. In the years to come, she would have tremendous influence over millions of people. If she recommended a book, the book would almost certainly end up on the bestseller list. If she said negative things about a particular food, sales of the food would plummet. She would help make legislation to aid in preventing child abuse. She would bring hope and encouragement to millions.

The woman climbed the podium and accepted her diploma. She waved it and spoke to her father in the audience. "See, Daddy, I amounted to something."

Indeed she has. Oprah Winfrey hosts the top-rated talk show in the United States. She is worth more than $340 million. She is the highest paid woman in show business and the first African-American woman to own her own studio.

Oprah at her college graduation ceremony.

Entertaining the Chickens

*O*prah Gail Winfrey was born January 29, 1954, on a farm near Kosciusko, Mississippi. Her mother, Vernita Lee, was only 18 years old when she had Oprah. She wanted to name her Orpah after a person in the Bible. However, there was a mistake by the person doing the birth certificate. They spelled the name "Oprah." Oprah has used that name ever since.

Vernita never married Oprah's father, an army soldier named Vernon Winfrey. At first, Vernita tried to find a job around Kosciusko. There were few jobs there, so she left Oprah with her own mother, Hattie Mae Lee. Vernita moved to Milwaukee, Wisconsin, to work as a maid. Oprah stayed with Hattie, her grandmother.

It was a lonely life for young Oprah. "The nearest neighbor was a blind man up the road," she said. "There weren't other kids... no playmates, no toys except for one corncob doll."

Oprah Winfrey

Oprah Winfrey at the 1999 National Book Awards.

There was always a lot of work to do on her grandmother's farm. One of Oprah's jobs was to help feed her grandmother's chickens, pigs, and cows. She enjoyed doing that. The animals soon became her friends. She talked to them and gave them parts in the games she made up. Later, she sang and danced for them.

Church was another big part of young Oprah's life. Each Sunday she and her grandmother dressed in their best clothes and went to church. The services lasted for hours. Oprah had to sit quietly all that time. She let her imagination run wild to help pass the time. She was always playing pretend games.

Oprah's grandmother was very strict. If Oprah misbehaved in any way, her grandmother would punish her. Often that meant she would strike Oprah with a switch. (A switch is a slender branch from a tree.) The whippings hurt Oprah badly. She would try to behave, but she always made mistakes. Hattie Mae believed children should be seen and not heard. Yet Oprah loved to talk and it was hard to keep her quiet.

One place Oprah could talk was at church. Hattie Mae encouraged her to recite poems. She did that very well. She became a popular person to ask to recite at church, teas, and recitals. Many people recognized she had a gift for it. They told her grandmother, "Hattie Mae, that child sure is gifted." Oprah loved it, too. She would get very excited when she heard someone say, "Little Miss Winfrey will now do her recitation."

Her grandmother also worked with her on her letters. Oprah was reading by the time she was only three years old. She learned to write soon after that. On her first day of kindergarten, she wrote the teacher a note. It said, "Dear Miss New, I do not think I belong here." She was right. The school officials moved her up to first grade. The following year she talked to them again. "I didn't think it was necessary to go to second grade," she said. "So I told my teacher and was moved into third grade. I couldn't stand to be bored."

Oprah Winfrey speaking at the 1999 National Book Awards dinner.

Problem Child

*W*hen Oprah was six years old, her mother decided she could take care of her. So Oprah moved to the big city of Milwaukee. It was very different from the farm. The farm had lots of room to roam. Now, she and her mother shared a room in another woman's house.

In the city, Oprah was tempted by all the things they couldn't afford. She saw pretty toys and dresses everywhere. Yet her mother did not have enough money to buy them for her. Worse still, her mother worked so hard that Oprah rarely saw her. She was not happy in Milwaukee. At that time, Vernita talked to Oprah's father. He had married and now lived in Nashville, Tennessee. Vernon and his wife, Zelma, said they would be happy to have Oprah come live with them.

Life with her father was much different. Vernon had many strict rules that he expected Oprah to follow. She had chores to do and Bible verses to memorize. Vernon worked with Oprah to improve her math skills.

Oprah Winfrey

Oprah hadn't been with her father long when her mother called again. Vernita was expecting another baby. She wanted Oprah to come join her and the new baby back in Wisconsin. She was living in a house of her own now.

Oprah was sad to leave her father and stepmother. She moved back to Milwaukee and her mother soon had a baby girl. Vernita named Oprah's half-sister Patricia Lee. Two years later, Oprah's half-brother Jeffrey was born. Now Oprah had to compete with two other kids for her mother's attention. She was unhappy about the situation and began to misbehave. She told lies and made up stories to get what she wanted, such as a new pair of glasses or a puppy.

Another tragic thing happened to Oprah in Milwaukee. When she was just nine years old, a 19-year-old cousin sexually abused her. Oprah didn't know what was happening to her at the time. She was afraid to tell anyone about it. She thought it was her fault.

Oprah Winfrey bites her lip as she testifies on child abuse in front of the Senate Judiciary Committee in Washington, D.C., in 1991.

Oprah Winfrey

Oprah's behavior kept getting worse. One day when she was about 13, she ran away from home. She stopped when she saw a fancy limousine. A famous singer was getting out of the limousine. Oprah ran up to her and told her that her family had abandoned her and she needed money to return home to Ohio. The singer was a woman named Aretha Franklin. She gave Oprah $100. Oprah used the money to spend the night in a hotel room.

Singer Aretha Franklin

Rules, Rules, & More Rules

*W*hen she was 14, Oprah became pregnant. Her baby died just a few days after birth. By now, Vernita was at her wit's end. She tried to have Oprah sent to a juvenile detention center but there was no room. She felt she had no choice but to send Oprah back to her father in Nashville.

"I'm grateful to my mother for sending me away," Oprah said. "If she hadn't, I would have taken an absolutely different path in life."

Back in Nashville, Oprah once again had to follow her father's strict rules. She couldn't wear short skirts anymore. She had to read a new book and do a book report about it every week. She had to pick new words out of the dictionary, learn their meanings, and recite them to him. She had to work in his grocery store. He told her she could not live with them unless she got A's in school.

Oprah Winfrey in the television series Brewster Place.

Oprah Winfrey

Fortunately, Oprah was gifted and intelligent. She began to put her mind to her studies and excelled at Nashville East High School. She took a public speaking class and honed her speaking skills. She also joined the school's drama club and acted in plays. Oprah loved being on stage. She memorized her lines as easily as she'd memorized poems back in Mississippi.

As a senior, the other students elected Oprah president of the student council. She also was invited to attend the White House Conference on Youth in Colorado. There she met high school student leaders from around the country. She also met President Richard Nixon. Later that year a speaking engagement took her to Los Angeles, California. She saw Hollywood and made up her mind she wanted her career to include speech and drama.

When she was 17, she entered the Miss Fire Prevention contest and won. "I entered it as a fluke," she said. "I was the only Negro in the contest. I certainly never expected to win because, why would I? And I won. I said I wanted to be a journalist, like Barbara Walters."

Local radio station WVOL had sponsored the contest. Oprah stopped by the station to pick up her prize, a watch. "One of the guys had a tape recorder. He asked me if I'd ever heard my voice on tape," she said. "When he heard my voice, he called in the news director. He said, 'Hey, listen to this kid read.'"

The station executives loved the sound of Oprah's voice. They hired her on the spot to read news and weather after school.

Oprah Winfrey at a concert by singer Tina Turner.

Oprah Winfrey

The Broadcast World

*T*he fall following graduation, Oprah started classes at Tennessee State University. She had won a scholarship to the school in a speech contest. By that time, she already had been working for the radio station for nearly six months. She was very busy with work and classes. Somehow she managed to squeeze in another contest—the Miss Black Tennessee pageant. "I didn't expect to win, nor did anyone else expect me to," she said. "There were all these light-skinned girls, and here I was, real dark-skinned." She impressed the judges with her talent, intelligence, and honesty. Oprah won that contest, too.

Soon Nashville television station WTVF-TV approached her about a job. They wanted her to become an anchorwoman. An anchorperson reads news and cuts between segments from reporters. Oprah pretended she was Barbara Walters when she auditioned for the job.

Oprah Winfrey

Oprah Winfrey

The station offered the position to Oprah, so she quit her job at the radio station and took the TV job. She was only 19 years old and ready for new experiences. There were many of those at the station.

"When I was doing television in Nashville, I was given a stand-in job for just one day. I was filling in on one of those local talk-show community-affairs programs that air at two in the morning. I remember...thinking this is what I'd like to do."

Even though Oprah was an adult with a regular job, her father still wanted her to follow his rules. She would joke she was the only anchorwoman who had to be home by 11 P.M.! She began to dream of a life on her own. Her chance came when she received a call from WJZ-TV in Baltimore, Maryland. They wanted her to be a co-anchor on their news broadcast. She was just two months shy of graduating from college, yet she accepted the job and moved to Baltimore.

Part of Oprah's job involved reporting as well as simply reading the news. She didn't enjoy that task. "I really wasn't cut out for the news," she said. "I'd have to fight back the tears if a story was too sad." Even though she didn't like the work, Oprah felt it was her duty to continue.

Fate stepped in nine months later when she was 22 years old. The station fired her from her co-anchor job and made her the host of a talk show. It was called *People Are Talking*. "They put me on the talk show just to get rid of me, but it was really my saving grace. The first day I did it, I thought, 'This is what I really should have been doing all along.'"

Oprah Winfrey with newscaster Barbara Walters.

A 1986 photo of Oprah Winfrey.

A Show of Her Own

*O*prah hosted *People Are Talking* for seven years. It became a very popular show. Yet Oprah wanted more. She dreamed of a bigger show in a bigger city. One day she heard from WLS-TV in Chicago, Illinois. They aired a show called *A.M. Chicago*. They offered her a chance to host the show.

Oprah jumped at the chance. She knew it would be a challenge because *A.M. Chicago* ran in the same time slot as *The Phil Donahue Show*. Plus, Oprah knew some people did not like African Americans just because they were African Americans. Never one to turn down a challenge, Oprah jumped in with both feet.

Within a year, Oprah had expanded the show's ratings and share by 50 percent. It wasn't long before WLS expanded *A.M. Chicago* from a half-hour to an hour show. Then they renamed it *The Oprah Winfrey Show*.

Presidential candidate George W. Bush appears on The Oprah Winfrey Show, *September 19, 2000.*

The next step would be for Oprah's show to go into syndication. Syndication means television stations around the country can carry a show. But the syndicator Oprah wanted couldn't do it because of the show's ownership. Oprah solved the problem by buying the show herself. *The Oprah Winfrey Show* went nationwide in 1986. Almost immediately, it became the number one daytime talk show in the United States. Oprah Winfrey became a household name.

Oprah still owns her show and now she produces it, too. In fact, she is the first African-American woman ever to own her own production studio. She named it Harpo Productions. Harpo is Oprah spelled backwards.

The Oprah Winfrey Show has won many awards, including 20 Emmy Awards. It reaches more than 15 million people each day. Oprah feels it's part of her mission on earth. "I'm really proud of this television show. Every day my intention is to empower people and my intention is for other people to recognize by watching our show that you really are responsible for your life. I think I can be a catalyst for people beginning to think more insightfully about themselves and their lives."

Oprah Winfrey joined Roger King, chairman of the board of King World, at a news conference in Chicago in 1985, where it was announced that The Oprah Winfrey Show *would be syndicated nationwide.*

A New Style of Talk Show

*I*n 1993-94, Oprah began to take a hard look at her TV show. Like most talk shows at the time, she had been discussing topics that many called sensational. Talk shows thrived on it. Each wanted to feature the most outrageous story or situation. People always were willing to air their dirty laundry on television.

Oprah decided it was time to stop talking about people's problems and start helping people solve them. She knew she was taking a risk in doing so. "We've grown in the past 10 years," she said. "And I want the show to reflect that growth. Even if our ratings go in the tank. I'm not going to be able to spend from now until the year 2000 talking to people about dysfunction. Yes, we are dysfunctional. Now, what are we willing to do to change it?"

First Lady Hillary Rodham Clinton appearing on The Oprah Winfrey Show.

She made the change and began to focus on tougher issues. She also looked at what people could do to make their lives better. At first, her ratings dropped. Then slowly, they began to go back up. She had never felt better about her work. "What really is the driving force for me now are those moments when I know that I've reached somebody."

She definitely has reached somebody. She receives about 5,000 letters a week. Some people even send her their bills in the hopes that she will pay them. There are even Oprah Winfrey chat rooms and web sites on the Internet.

Rosie O'Donnell appearing on The Oprah Winfrey Show.

Michael Jordan and Oprah Winfrey
share a laugh during a taping of
The Oprah Winfrey Show.

Making Movies

Oprah always enjoyed being on stage. Just
before her show went national, she received a call
from Hollywood movie director Steven Spielberg. He
was making a movie from the book *The Color Purple*.
The Color Purple was one of Oprah's favorite books.
She had wanted to be in a movie version of the book
ever since she read it. She was thrilled when
Spielberg asked her if she'd like to audition for a part
in the movie.

She auditioned and won the part of Sofia, an
abused wife. The filming was one of her favorite
experiences of her life. "I was really depressed when
we finished," she said. "It was the best experience I
ever had in my life. I felt never in my life will I be
able to top those feelings.

Oprah acted the part so well she received an
Academy Award nomination in 1986 for Best
Supporting Actress. She went on to perform in
several other movies, including *The Women of
Brewster Place.*

Oprah Winfrey hugs fellow cast member Tina Majorino as they arrive for the premiere of Before Women Had Wings.

The Women of Brewster Place has a special place in Oprah's heart. The movie is based on a book Oprah read while filming *The Color Purple*. Oprah loved the book. "The book makes a great statement for maintaining your dignity in a world that tries to strip you of it," she said. Immediately, she wanted to make a movie of it.

It took years for Oprah to convince a network to take on the project. Finally, ABC-TV agreed to make it into a mini-series. *Brewster Place* eventually became the first film to be co-produced by Harpo, Oprah's own studio. It aired in 1989 and featured Oprah in the starring role. It was one of the highest rated mini-series that season.

Oprah and Harpo made more broadcast history in 1993. Oprah interviewed Michael Jackson live from his ranch in California. More than 90 million people watched the 90-minute program. It was the fourth most watched entertainment special in television history.

Oprah Winfrey with
Michael Jackson.

Personal Battles

*P*art of Oprah's appeal to viewers is how freely she shares her personal experiences. She has talked on television about how she was abused as a child. On a show about drug abuse, she admitted she had taken drugs under pressure from a man she was dating. All of these revelations make her audience feel like she's their close friend.

For example, in May 1997, Oprah called a woman. The woman had won a contest to see Tina Turner in concert. When Oprah said who she was, the woman got very excited. "This is *my* Oprah?" the woman yelled. "My Oprah!"

Two of the biggest personal battles Oprah has shared with her audience are her abuse and her weight. Oprah was physically abused by her family many times. She also suffered sexual abuse at the hands of friends and family members. "I blamed myself," she said. "I was always very needy, always in need of attention, and they just took advantage of that. There were people, certainly, around me who were aware of it, but they did nothing."

Oprah Winfrey hosted the
Emmy Awards in 1992.

Her weight also has been the topic of many shows. She spent many years dieting only to regain the weight. Worst of all, every time she gained weight it became a public event. "One day I ordered apple pancakes in a restaurant and read about it in two newspapers the next day," she said.

Finally, she realized why she overate. "I ruled my life by what other people wanted me to do," she said. "It was an emotional problem that manifested itself physically. I never really allowed myself to feel anything because I covered it up with food."

In the summer of 1992, Oprah weighed more than 230 pounds. She felt terrible about herself. She remembers hosting the Emmy Awards and being ashamed of how she looked. After the awards, she left for a spa in Colorado. There she met a personal trainer named Bob Greene. She has been working with him ever since.

Oprah Winfrey shows off her new figure in Chicago, November 15, 1988. She credited her 67-pound (30.4 kg) weight loss to a liquid diet and exercise. She now maintains her weight at around 150 pounds (68 kg).

Greene helped her understand how her emotions surrounding food were adding to her weight problem. He coached Oprah to learn why it was she ate. Oprah learned to stop using food for comfort. He also started her on a rigorous, regular running program. In 1994, she ran the Marine Corps marathon in Washington, D.C. It was a very proud moment for her. "This is better than an Emmy," she said.

Today, Oprah maintains her weight at around 150 pounds. She still has to work at it. She runs every day and eats a sensible diet. Her success continues to inspire others to do the same.

"It's not a weight-loss program as much as a get-fit and get-moving program," she said. "I've been through every diet under the sun, and I can tell you the getting up, getting out, and walking is always the first goal."

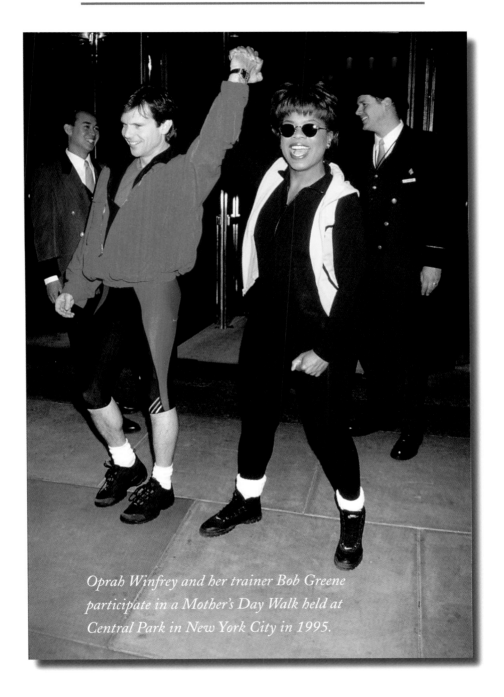

Oprah Winfrey and her trainer Bob Greene participate in a Mother's Day Walk held at Central Park in New York City in 1995.

Writing Books

*O*prah always loved to read. She also has taken on the challenge of writing books. Her struggles with her weight have led to writing two books.

In 1993, after she began working with Greene, she also began working with chef Rosie Daley. She shared Rosie's low-fat recipes in a book. She titled it *In the Kitchen with Rosie*. The book became the fastest-selling book of all time and has sold more than 6.5 million copies.

In 1996, Oprah worked with Green to write *Make the Connection: Ten Steps to a Better Body—and a Better Life*. The book combines tips for losing and keeping off weight with Oprah's personal story. It, too, has reached the ranks of bestseller.

Oprah also started Oprah's Book Club on her TV show. Any book she picks for her club is bound to become a bestseller. She's just happy that people are interested. "The best thing about it is the thousands of letters from people who haven't picked up a book in 20 years," she said. The publishing industry gave Oprah an LMP Award for her work promoting books. She is the first person outside the publishing industry to win the award.

Wearing her newly-presented gold medal, Oprah Winfrey holds up her National Book Awards trophy in New York City, November 17, 1999. She received a special 50th Anniversary Gold Medal for her contribution to reading and books.

Giving Back

Oprah frequently tells her viewers how they can make their lives better. She also encourages them to help others. It's no surprise that Oprah does her share to help people, too.

In 1986, she formed a Big Sister group with 24 teenage girls from the Cabrini-Green Housing Project in Chicago. Never one to mince words, Oprah gave them her usual straight talk.

"When we talk about goals, they say they want Cadillacs. I say, 'If you cannot talk correct, if you cannot read or do math, if you become pregnant, if you drop out of school, you will never have a Cadillac. And if you get any D's or F's on your report card, you're out of this group. Don't tell me you want to do great things in your life if all you carry to school is a radio!'"

Oprah also started a scholarship program at Tennessee State University. She named it after her father. The Vernon Winfrey Scholarship Fund gives scholarships to 10 TSU students each year.

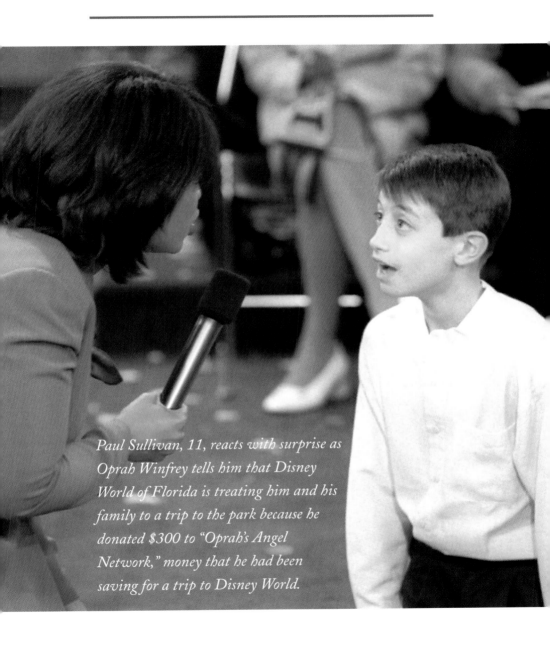

Paul Sullivan, 11, reacts with surprise as Oprah Winfrey tells him that Disney World of Florida is treating him and his family to a trip to the park because he donated $300 to "Oprah's Angel Network," money that he had been saving for a trip to Disney World.

In 1991, Oprah started another crusade. The death of a four-year-old Chicago girl horrified her. A convicted child molester killed the girl. Oprah set the wheels in motion for a new law. It was called the National Child Protection Act. The law created a database of convicted child abusers and molesters. Employers could check the backgrounds of people applying to work with children to make sure they didn't have a record of harming children. Thanks in large part to Oprah, the bill became law in December 1993.

Earlier in 1993, Oprah filmed a TV movie called *There Are No Children Here*. It was about black families in a Chicago housing project. Oprah donated the money she made from the film to fund scholarships for housing project residents. She also founded a non-profit foundation called Families for a Better Life. The foundation helps families by sponsoring them to get jobs and homes outside the housing projects.

On a personal level, Oprah has helped her family through the years with gifts of cars and money. Yet it frustrates her that some of them are unwilling to help themselves. "I realized you cannot buy people their personal freedom," she said. "No matter how much you do, there is always an excuse."

Oprah Winfrey shakes hands with President Clinton, center, as former Presidents George Bush, right, and Gerald Ford, left, look on at the close of the President's Call to Action rally during the Presidents' Summit for America's Future in 1997.

What's Next for Oprah?

*O*prah divides her time among her apartment in Chicago, her farm in Indiana, a ranch in Colorado, and a home near Miami, Florida. She lives with her fiance since 1992, Stedman Graham. She also spends lots of time with her nine dogs and her personal trainer, Bob Greene.

Many people pester Oprah about when she and Stedman will marry. She says they will marry when they're ready. As of yet, she says neither of them are. They each maintain busy personal and professional lives. They also enjoy each other's company.

Oprah likes to tell about how they began dating. "At first, I wasn't really that interested," she said. "He's so handsome. I figured, if he's calling me, either he's a jerk or there's something wrong with him.

"He called three times... The first time I stood him up. The second time I made excuses. Finally, the third time, he said, 'I'm not going to ask you anymore.' So I went out with him."

Oprah Winfrey with her longtime companion Stedman Graham.

The next day, she told her co-workers about their date. "I'm so glad I went! He bought me roses, paid for dinner, and was interested in what I had to say!"

Oprah also has expressed that she might not continue doing her television show. After all these years, she often dreams of doing something different. Something totally different.

"I dream about finding a new way of doing television that elevates us all," she said. "My goal for myself is to reach the highest level of humanity that is possible to me. Then, when I'm done, when I quit the planet, I want to be able to say, 'Boy, I did that, didn't I? Yes I did!'

"And I want to get up there and high-five with the angels. High-five with them and have them say, 'Yes girl, you did it. You really did it!'"

Oprah Winfrey poses for photographers at a party celebrating the first anniversary of her "O" magazine on April 17, 2001, in New York City.

Timeline

January 29, 1954: Oprah Gail Winfrey born on a farm near Kosciusko, Mississippi.

1971: Hired by radio station WVOL to read news and weather after school.

1973: Becomes first black anchorperson at television station WTVF-TV in Nashville, TN.

1976: Becomes co-anchor at WJZ-TV in Baltimore, MD.

1977: Becomes host of talk show *People Are Talking* at WJZ-TV.

1984: Hired by television station WLS-TV in Chicago, IL, to host *A.M. Chicago*, later renamed *The Oprah Winfrey Show*.

1985: Nominated for Academy Award for Best Supporting Actress for her role as Sofia in Steven Spielberg's *The Color Purple*.

1986: *The Oprah Winfrey Show* goes into nationwide syndication, quickly becoming the number one daytime talk show in the United States.

1988: Receives diploma from Tennessee State University.

1991: Initiates National Child Protection Act, which helps track convicted child abusers and molesters. Signed into law by President Clinton in 1993.

1998: Stars as Sethe in the critically acclaimed movie *Beloved*.

2000: Starts her own magazine, *O, The Oprah Magazine*.

Where on the Web?

http://www.oprah.com/
The official site for Oprah Winfrey.

**http://mrshowbiz.go.com/celebrities/
people/oprahwinfrey/bio.html**
Mr. Showbiz bio of Oprah.

**http://talkshows.about.com/cs/
oprahwinfrey/**
News and photo archives from About.com.

**http://www.eonline.com/Facts/People/
Bio/0,128,16930,00.html**
A profile of Oprah from E!Online.

**http://www.time.com/time/time100/
artists/profile/winfrey.html**
An online profile from TIME magazine.

Glossary

anchor

The person on a TV news show who reads the news or introduces the news reports.

audition

To try out for a part in a play or movie.

catalyst

Something that brings about a change in something else.

commencement

The graduation exercises of a school or college.

dysfunction

When something is not functioning the way it should.

syndication

A business that sells a TV show to many other TV stations.

Oprah Winfrey addresses the crowd at a memorial service at Yankee Stadium, September 23, 2001. Thousands were at the stadium to mourn the victims of the September 11th attack on the World Trade Center in New York City.

Index

A
A.M. Chicago 32

B
Baltimore, MD 29
Big Sister 52

C
Cabrini-Green
  Housing Project 52
California 23, 42
Chicago, IL 32, 52,
  54, 56
Colorado 23, 46, 56

E
Emmy Awards 34, 46

F
Families for a Better
  Life 54
Florida 56
Franklin, Aretha 19

G
Greene, Bob 46, 48,
  50, 56
Graham, Stedman 56

H
Hollywood, CA 23,
  40

I
Illinois 32
In the Kitchen with
  Rosie 50
Indiana 56

J
Jackson, Michael 42
Jeffrey (half-brother)
  16

K
Kosciusko, Mississippi
  8

L
Lee, Hattie Mae 8
LMP Award 50
Los Angeles, CA 23

M
Make the Connection:
  Ten Steps to a Better
  Body—and a Better
  Life 50
Marine Corps
  marathon 48
Maryland 29
Miami, FL 56
Milwaukee, WI
  8, 14, 16
Miss Black Tennessee
  26
Miss Fire Prevention
  23
Mississippi 8, 23

N
Nashville, TN 14, 20,
  23, 26, 29
Nashville East High
  School 23
National Child
  Protection Act 54
Nixon, Richard 23

O
Orpah 8

P
Patricia Lee (half
  sister) 16
People Are Talking
  30, 32

S
Oprah's Book Club
  50
Spielberg, Steven 40

T
Tennessee 4, 14, 26,
  52
Tennessee State
  University
  4, 26, 52
The Color Purple
  40, 42
The Oprah Winfrey
  Show 32, 34
The Phil Donahue
  Show 32
The Women of Brewster
  Place 40, 42
There Are No Children
  Here 54

U
United States 6, 34

V
Vernita (mother)
  8, 14, 16, 20
Vernon Winfrey
  Scholarship Fund
  52

W
Washington, D.C. 48
White House
  Conference on
  Youth 23
Winfrey, Vernon 8,
  14, 52
Winfrey, Zelma 14
Wisconsin 8, 16
WJZ 29
WLS 32
WTVF 26
WVOL 24